Meditations
From the Muck

BY NAHSHON COOK

ISBN: 978-1-7374655-2-2

Introduction

Dear One,

Hello! It's been suggested to me that I write an introduction
to this collection for readers who are new to my work. So
here it is:

Yesterday, I was talking on the phone with a sister-friend who
asked me how I was doing. I told her, "I'm just trying to be
a horseman in my heart." That's what this book, *Meditations
From the Muck*, is about.

Thank you for buying it, thank you for reading it, and may
it a blessing to you, the horses, and the humans in your life.

Peace and a smile,
   Nahshon Cook.

1

This morning, while cleaning stalls, I thought about being an ancestor in the making, and how, one day, a beautiful herd of healthy horses will gallop out of my chest until this life's last breath leaves another vacant body behind like the memory of a moment in time.

2

This morning, while cleaning stalls, I thought about how learning to be as happy as my least happy horse has made it possible for me to see that I can't stop what I don't first understand.

Not being able to stop what I don't first understand has helped me see my intention as the angel of my action.

Seeing my intention as the angel of my action has taught me how profound an act of love and safekeeping listening deeply to my horses is.

Practicing how profound an act of love and safekeeping listening deeply to my horses is is how I learned to follow the horse and find heaven in every step.

3

This morning, while cleaning stalls, I thought about what my sale add would look like if I were a horse. My price, my age, my vices, etc.

The only thing I could come up with was:
Free to a good home.

4

This morning, while cleaning stalls, I thought about how I'm not completely sure of what a prayer is,

but every time I say one the response I receive is a choice and the time to make it,

like how cleaning my horse's stalls every morning and every night keeps me closely connected to my center.

My center is where I communicate with horses in my body, but I can't connect with a horse without a horse to connect to.

And what is a connection if not each one knowing that they matter enough to be loved by the other one.

We lose our connection to the ones whose love we take for granted. Maintenancelessness is the hospice where relationships go to die.

5

This morning, while cleaning stalls, I thought about how, when I'm riding a horse, I sometimes imagine I'm white water rafting, and I'm balancing on this small inflatable rubber boat floating down the river by moving from inside of the horse's movement.

Then, like I tell myself all of the time: *The purpose of the journey is not fighting for freedom, but seeing that you're already free.*

I learn a lot about who I am from the time I spend with horses. I love horses deeply. Their teachings on emotional intelligence are salvation in the earth for me. I love people too, but I'm a lot more chill about it.

I often think of the universe as people bringing life back into themselves by looking out at the world and seeing something new every day. This is how I'm unlearning to be afraid. It's a beautiful meditation.

6

Last night, right before I went to bed, someone messaged me a meme that had two horses talking to each other about their people.

One said: Is your person a rescue too?

The other said: Yes, she's got issues, but we're working on it.

This morning, while cleaning stalls, I thought about some of the lessons I'm currently learning from my little herd of rescues.

Nova: See that little beam of light shining out from you heart, keep following it.

Remi: Sometimes you just need to be left alone to allow yourself to un-scatter so that all the pieces can fall into their proper place.

Mohawk: Sometimes you just need to allow yourself to be helped so that you can gather the scattered pieces and put them in their proper place.

Yoda-pony: Thank you. Just, thank you.

Dancer: Let's get on with it. We've got a life to live.

7

This morning, while cleaning stalls, I thought about the lady who walked into one of my clinics and, after I asked how I could help, said she and her horse needed I couples counseling.

"I'm a horseman," I said.

"Then I need you to be an advocate for the horse," she said.

I said, "What's going on?"

"He's a good horse," she said, "very highly trained. But, he and I aren't clicking with each other."

I said, "Are you his person?"

She began to cry and said, "No."

Just then, the horse turned and looked at her like 'See, I told you', then walked towards the arena gate and waited for the lady to open it so that they could leave.

She said, "Okay then, that's it."

"Well," I said, "now, if he where my horse, my job would be to find him the right home. You can choose to do whatever you want with that feedback."

Every love doesn't last for always.

8

This morning, while cleaning stalls, I scooped poop into the muck bucket while trying to wrap my mind around all that will happen next year, and all that has happened this year, and what a gift this precious human birth is.

9

This morning, while cleaning stalls, I thought about how trusting life so that life is trustworthy is intuition, which teaches you how to trust yourself, and you believe in you enough to stay more present to the world with an open heart.

That staying present to the world is teaching me how to trust the world, and as the world becomes more trustworthy, more and more kindred spirits have begun to appear. And all because my horses are teaching me to stay out of my own way enough to trust them so that they can be trustworthy.

I'm beginning to see that the trustworthiness, that my horses are teaching me, is the art of living in creation instead of survival. It's how I'm learning to allow fear to show me where I'm disconnected and the way back to connection.

10

This morning, while cleaning stalls, I thought about how being with horses has taught me how to be with horses, and people too, and how we only really learn how to love ourselves in relationship with others.

I thought about how profoundly simple, and compassionate, and patient horses have been with me learning how to let them help me help them feel better...

I thought about how horses have taught me how damaging only asking questions you already know the answer to is, like someone who is happy being unhappy because that's the only life they were taught to live.

I thought about how horses are teaching me how to move out of my own mind enough to understand that I can't heal the hurts I'm addicted to, and that when I play with my emotions in such a way that my brain works differently to the point that my mind thinks healthy thoughts, then I'm able to see how to build the horses back from their brokenness, and myself too.

Horses have taught me how to love people by allowing me to love them, which is myself... where words are magic, and sentences cause effects like spells. This switch is sometimes rough, but it's easier for me now than it was before.

Horses are teaching me how to create myself so that I don't have to survive myself. Most times, it's as simple as softly singing a song, or whistling, which is also meditation

11

This morning, while cleaning stalls, I thought about bound-aries, and so asked Yoda-pony what his definition of healthy boundaries would be for him.

Yoda-pony said, "Pro me first."

12

This morning, while cleaning stalls, I thought about how B. and I were out to dinner at La Casita when I asked him what his first intimate memory was.

He said: Being a little boy with my head resting on my mom's lap while she ran her fingers through my hair.

13

This morning, while cleaning stalls, I thought about how my small herd is helping me see that evolution is found in every decision you make, and that compassion for others is also found in not straying too far away from the most difficult parts of one's own self.

When Yoda-pony first arrived at my stable, his mind was like a play about someone who'd built a room they'd locked themselves inside of all alone, because that's the only way they learned to trust being in relationship. But the room is part of a set design, so there were still faded patches of light shinning through like old memories.

The room is on a theater stage, so it doesn't look as real from the outside as it does on the inside. But still, it's full of unresolved contradictions: there's a two-by-four blocking the door, the low basement level windows at the base of the walls, the random rocking chair and dinning table, the set of purple stairs to nowhere. A blue tea cup saucer with a freshly cut piece of pumpkin pie in the middle of the floor....

The crazy thing about living inside a mind like that is you can never see the castles crumbling down around you. But when everything is on the floor in pieces, and all you're left with are of remnants of what was, you realize there's no life for you to live in that place anymore.

Yoda-pony felt far enough away from his past last April when he asked me to please leave him alone because he was deciding whether or not he wanted to leave his body.

Last September, I had a student come with her horse from Minnesota to study with me for a week. On the first day, before she left, she walking into the arena and told me she'd just checked in with Yoda-pony, and the he told her he was still decided whether or not her wanted to leave his body, and that he appreciated the space.

14

This morning, while cleaning stalls, I thought about how the thing I love most about my work with horses is that I can care enough to share enough of what is real about myself so that there's someone else on the other end of the conversation to listen to,

like an honest, emotionally safe friend who's also willing to talk about their mental health, and their doubts, and their imperfections, and how weird life in the world sometimes feels...

All of the shit that makes it possible for true connection to blossom beautifully like a fuchsia orchid into a healthy relationship's ability to appease the apologizer by accepting their apology and the disregard still not be okay.

15

This morning, while cleaning stalls, I thought about the video my friend sent me from her reservation of two wild horses coming up into the field with her saddle horses.

The saddle horse's bodies told the story of a life lived in time and space where the present moment is full of old thoughts fighting for the survival of past feelings.

The wild horse's bodies told the story of a life lived in energy where the present moment is full of new feelings fighting for the creation of future thoughts.

I saw myself in the saddle horses walking up to their people. I saw myself the wild horses with no people to walk up to.

16

This morning, while cleaning stalls, I thought about how my horses are teaching me that stress means needing to be afraid of what you know. Anxiety means needing to be afraid of what you don't know.

Needing to be afraid means the fear of letting go. Letting go means not needing to be afraid.

I thought about how my horses are teaching me how horses aren't afraid of being soft for people who are soft.

Being a soft person means not forcing time.

Because soft people spend their time not forcing time, rather than forcing time, horses aren't afraid to change.

Not forcing time means understanding.
Forcing time means not understanding.
Change is the journey between remembering and forgetting.

Understanding means remembering to gather the scattered pieces of the puzzle and taking each step to put each piece in its proper place.

Not understanding means forgetting that a complete puzzle isn't made up of missing pieces.

17

This morning, while cleaning stalls, I though about the magpie who sometimes sits on the top of Yoda-pony's mane and sings him lullabies in the afternoon while he's out sunbathing in his paddock.

18

This morning, while cleaning stalls, I thought about how the word horse-person looks like it means a person who follows horses.

And how, for me, following horses is how I find heaven in every step.

And how, for me, heaven is the experiential reality of holiness in the present moment.

And how, for me, the experiential reality of holiness in the present moment is where life lives.

19

This morning, while cleaning stalls, I thought about how when you look at a horse, and see that horse, you can recognize their person, and how one of the magic places horses hold for me is the space that's created for them to teach me something about myself with their answers to my questions.

And I thought about how horses have really helped me understand that the rules are created by the players of the game; and how the players of the game are all just trying to make sense of the lesson they each learned about loving themselves from past relationships with others.

20

This morning, while cleaning stalls, I thought about my life as the shortest longest time that I have, and how I love spending as much of it as possibly I can on being an equidtrovert

in the my barn deepening my understanding of how I can only be what I want to be when who I am becomes the experience of what I want be

by diagnosing a pattern that needs to change before beginning to think and act in the direction of a pattern's change until the needed change happens.

If a horse wants my help, this is how I help the horse. It's how I help myself, too, when I want help. Everything is practice for everything else.

21

This morning, while cleaning stalls, I thought about how someone who'd read one of my previous meditations sent me a message saying that my writing sounded like I needed some fresh air because I was breathing in too much methane gas.

That person's words made me laugh so hard I cried. They reminded me of something my Grandpa told me about how hard it would be for me to reach my full potential if I stayed stuck in being too self-conscious.

All of my horses arrived in my life as a great opportunity to learn disguised as an impossible problem to solve that is teaching me how to intentionally change my awareness when I want to change what my energy does.

Every highlight with each member of my herd has been nothing more than a bunch of lowlights lit by the flame I've found in the nothing moments of my time with them...just doing what I do to care for them, as lovingly as I can, everyday.

I've come to understand that flame as the miracle of letting go of self-limiting beliefs and trusting what's left, which is always only me living life in the present moment.

22

This morning, while cleaning stalls, I thought about what more life wants from me. So I asked, and this is what I got:

To keep letting horses teach you that when you take it one step at a time, the next step always arrives.

23

This morning, while cleaning stalls, I thought about how sometimes, still, when I offer Yoda-pony my hand, he'll tense a little bit, and I can see in his eyes that he wants to be hugged, but really can't stand to be touched.

I often look at Yoda-pony and imagine him to be the returned Chinese seer of people and things who wrote the beautifully simple proverb that says, "Hard times make for good poetry."

The first time I read that, I realized that poems only happen where life is. And how, sometimes, living feels like I'm in the right chapter, but on the wrong page, and that's why I can't seem to find the answer to my question in this particular collection of words.

24

This morning, while cleaning stalls, I thought about belief as a narrative you keep telling yourself over and over again in your mind and heart until it is true for you.

I thought about how belief is created by the enlightening experience of a divine revelation or a theoretical education, both of which being a horseman are for me.

25

This morning, while cleaning stalls, I thought about how my horses have taught me that they're afraid of my ambition more than they are afraid of me.

Ambition is an addiction to doing that turns my mind into stone, like bone-on-bone arthritis. All of the cartilage is gone, and it's really hard for thoughts to move.

26

This morning, while cleaning stalls, I thought about why I love being with my horses. But, I often wonder who I am that my horses love being with me.

I thought about how people study what we don't have enough of, so that we can figure out where to find it, so that we can get more.

And this is the most beautiful lesson I've learned from my horses so far: that relationship, simply defined, means You are important to me.

What are my horses, if not my teachers? What am I, if not my horses' job.

To open yourself completely to another while calmly staying grounded in yourself is connection. This, I think, is the key: I can hear you when you see me.

27

This morning, while cleaning stalls, I thought about how I love that horses are teaching me how to stop living out of old arguments that are afraid of moving the story into where life is right now.

I thought about how I love that horses are teaching me that one's truth is an authentic identity, not a traditional image, and how techniques are only as helpful as their results.

I thought about how horses are teaching me how to not listen to what someone appears to be, so that I can hear who they are.

28

This morning, while cleaning stalls, I thought about Lungta, the spirit-horse of the Himalayas, whose hoof sounds are a seeker's secret snapping of flag prayers for peace and prosperity of all beings in the earth galloping across the sky.

I thought about Lungta as awareness, and the different levels of the aspirant's ability to understand that energy follows insight, like karma making clear that compassion for others is the heart of people not being afraid to care for the most profoundly disturbed parts of their own selves with great love.

I thought about how this work with my horses has taught me that my own heart is the only true shelter for prayer in my life.

29

This morning, while cleaning stalls, I thought about my work with horses as prayer.

I thought about prayer as believing.

I thought about believing as giving.

I thought about giving as letting go.

I thought about letting go as surrender.

I thought about surrender as prayer.

I feel prayer happen inside of me when I work with horses.

My prayer is an extension of me.

My work with horses is an extension of my prayer.

I thought about how belief is education.

30

This morning, while cleaning stalls, I thought about how it, sometimes, feels like there's a kill pen full of horses hoping for help in my mind. Their pain is the past catching up with the future, and coming harder than thought possible, like a mother whose child you've hurt.

I thought about horses exploding or imploding instead of going numb and shutting down while being worked by some person who was taught to make themselves too big to be heard when they wanted to be seen.

I had a former student who owned a lovely first-rate young horse who was the color of the sun. One day this person had decided she'd spent enough time in my barn to feel safe enough to tell me how she thought I was wasting my time and talent with my rescues.

But, my rescues have held my hand and guided me through the very real process of rehabbing their broken bodies from nearing the end of life and back into beautiful poems of bio-mechanics and energy.

31

This morning, while cleaning stalls, I thought about how grateful I am for my horses, and little magic Yoda-pony.

When I'm with them it's like like the gates of heaven open up.

I'm in awe of the way my horses have offered their lives to my life like a healer, led by the spirit, who's teaching me how holiness means loving all of myself enough to know that I am worthy of receiving love;

and that meditation means energy following imagination like a shadow;

and that transformation means ceasing to exist inside of self-limiting beliefs;

and that change is the journey between what was and what will be.

32

This morning, while cleaning stalls, I thought about what type of person I would find if I went further inside of myself, and how thinking either hurts or helps depending on which thoughts are followed, and by whom, and to where.

I thought about how thought is like an artist creating art without worrying about what the other thinkers will think when they experience it.

Way deep down in the ground of my being where light does not reach and left over lifetimes occur, there is a formless, nameless energy radiating from the space between cause and effect like the universe.

A journey is choices. You either do it and you do it, or you don't and you don't. Being with horse is as far as I've gotten.

33

This morning, while cleaning stalls, I thought about how, for me, helping other people's horses get better is great, but it's my personal horses getting better that lets me know I'm not a failure.

They've taught me the difference between being patient enough to allow the horse to teach me how to offer a relationship that they will accept, and not knowing how to trust the horse's intelligence to lead me to the reality of their progress not being possible if the only thing that I change is their condition and not myself;

there's a lot of personal power that's realized by unlearning how to be afraid of our fears, healing past hurts, and choosing not to respond from an unhealthy mind-space.

They've taught me that trust also means that everything that's known doesn't have to be explained.

34

This morning, while cleaning stalls, I thought about a person always wanting more from the horse than they already have, and how that makes the horse's life quite stressful. Sometimes, the horse's mental shock is so disturbing that just thinking about the past sends their adrenaline soaring.

My practice of the horse allowing me to help the horse heal is a meditation on me keeping the horse above my ambition.

My life with the horse as meditation has taught me to see change as energy shifts in the body, and the body as re-memory.

I think of the body as re-memory being the place from which we answer questions from the world around us is a beautiful definition of Feel.

35

This morning, while cleaning stalls, I thought about how listening to, and caring for, and being with my little herd of equid-angels makes me feel like life.

I thought about how following the horse and finding heaven in every step feels like I'm living inside of God's dream for me. It's my prayer.

I don't pray to change things. I pray to change me until things change.

36

This morning, while cleaning stalls, I thought about how I help the horses that want my help being put back together again. This is as far as I've gotten:

Feel the hurt
Lessen the pain

rest

Lessen the pain
Open the mind

rest

Open the mind
Correct the movement

rest

Correct the movement
Strengthen the body

rest

Strengthen the body
Rewire the brain

rest

Rewire the brain
Heal the hurt

37

This morning, while cleaning stalls, I looked in Nova's hay sack and saw how he'd eaten a cave into the middle of his dinner flakes that looked like the silhouetted entrance of a barn swallow's nest.

Leslie Desmond said horses do that to be nourished by the forage that the outside hasn't touched yet, like the endless spring of love and hope and appreciation and reverence that I have for those from the mysterious tribe of equid angels who make their way to me.

They've taught me how broken bodies, and broken hearts, and broken minds relearning to give birth to healthy movement is a journey into finding who will be left at the end.

38

This morning, while cleaning stalls, I thought about how yesterday someone wrote me saying that they respected the trust, and hope, and dedication, and good will I show to my horses.

I said, I give to the horses in my care what I want the horses in my care to give to me.

This person said, *I bet they feel that.*

I said, They do. That's why the work I do with them works. They know I love them beyond expectation, which seems to be the reason they improve in ways that exceed other people's expectation.

I thought about all that my horses have taught me about love: That it's hard, but that it's fun. And since it's fun, I usually don't realize the struggle until it's over.

39

This morning, while cleaning stalls, I thought about how I want to be

so relaxed in my work of helping hurt horses heal

that horses feel safe enough to be comfortable

with growth meaning keeping what helps and letting the rest go

as they journey to wholeness from their battle against brokenness

while holding space for the horse from the place of knowing

that I'll only be there to help the horse

get the most meaningful results from her or his efforts to live

for as long as the horse wants me to and for as long as I'm able

that what I am doing will only bring benefit to the horse

40

This morning, while cleaning stalls, I thought about how I don't understand it all.

But, if I look at a horse that wants my help as if that horse was me, I know what it's like to be that horse,

and the horse begins teaching me how to ask questions that it feels safe enough inside of to try and answer.

Sometimes, it feels like I'm the universe, and the horse's voice is the voice of God getting through to my heart.

41

This morning, while cleaning stalls, I thought about sentience and how hard of a time so many people have with the existence of a thing without their permission.

I thought about being with horses has taught me how to re-sentientize myself.

I thought about all of the beliefs about myself that I had to let go of to allow horses and other humans to be feeling beings in my world again.

I thought about the process of learning to trust that feeling is, and that feelings are, safe. And that it's okay to have feelings.

42

This morning, while cleaning stalls, I thought about how riding horses over jumps and traveling on a plane are almost the same in that falling feels like flying until you land.

43

This morning, while cleaning stall, I thought about clients controlling the market by what they pay for as permission for whatever the trainer is doing to horses to continue being done to horses, and about how much easier it is to complain than it is to change. That said, I'm thankful for the people who see themselves in me becoming the dream that life dreamed me to be enough to support my work.

I thought about the earth like it was my mare Mohawk, who was sold to the kill buyer at auction for having a body/mind connection that was broken down so badly that it was nearly uninhabitable for her anymore.

The people who sold her, I imagine, most likely, then went in search of another talented young horse to discover and destroy.

The people who saved her remind me of that quote by James Baldwin where he says, "Love has never been a popular movement, no one's ever wanted really to be free. The world is held together, is really held together, by the love and the passion of a very few people."

44

This morning, while cleaning stalls, I thought about how people treat horses like enemies by not allowing them adequate amount of time and space to respond in a relaxed, intention-filled breath way.

I thought about how being treated like an enemy is why resistance is a useful thing, until it isn't.

I thought about how learning to be with horses is a journey with levels like a computer game: you don't get to the next level until you pass the previous level,

where failure looks like horses telling you, in a gut-filling whisper-warning, that if you feel safe enough to trust yourself inside of the question you're being asked to answer, you'd know that you're walking in the wrong direction.

And that if you keep on in this way, you're going to run into a dangerous place where you're inner-peace is no longer more powerful than you're need to be right.

45

This morning, while cleaning stalls, I thought about how my zodiac sign is a centaur, and how I was born on the Feast Day of Epona, a Celtic Goddess who is the patron saint of equids and the people who love them.

I thought about how once someone, at one of my clinics, told me a story about an order of priests that Christianity had wiped out during the Spanish Reformation.

These priests took care of a herd of local horses, whom the priests believed had human souls. Anyway, she went on to say how the priests had received a letter from one of the Church higher-ups ordering them to destroy the horses.

The abbot of the order respond to his superiors with a letter that said, "There are no horses here." The priests didn't see themselves as separate from horses—on an energetic level."

46

This morning, while cleaning stalls, I thought about some of the horses I've met who would act crazy to make people stop hurting them. These horses weren't crazy, but they would act crazy to try and save themselves.

People would treat these horses like they were unreachable, and so these horses would usually just end up getting tossed around to worse and worse trauma inducing coma attempts.

I thought about how people teach these horses to be terrible by not touching them in a safe way, and how I wished no horse ever had the opportunity to be taught how to be terrible by people who are afraid of not having control.

I thought about how my work with these particular horses has taught me that when we mind what's happening to each other we begin to matter to each other, and care moves beyond the realm of needing to control one another by what we use to numb our own pain.

47

This morning, while cleaning stalls, I thought about what my work of listening to horses, and hearing them, and letting them know that what they said matters has taught me.

This is the heart of it: that apologies for our mistakes are only real when we learn enough to stop making the same mistakes, and that without love none of us are possible.

Now, love for horses, to me, has begun to look like people learning to care for horses better by starting them later, and teaching them much more slowly and correctly, so that they have longer, healthier, lifetimes in their bodies as the best friends that some of us have ever known.

48

This morning, while cleaning stalls, I thought about how as the plane I was on began its descent into Aukland I needed to throw away the two bananas that I had or else be heavily fined once I got to customs in Middle Earth.

When one of the flight attendants came to collect them, she asked if I wanted to learn to teach a small child learn to like eating banana. Thinking of my nieces, I said sure. So she took one of the bananas and said:

One: Peel the skin halfway down the banana in three sections.

Two: Bite the top quarter of the pulp off (in the instance, she broke the top off and threw it in the trash bag.)

Three: Lift the crowned middle peel from the back of the banana, and lay it over the space of the bitten off piece.
Four: Look, a penguin.

I laughed so hard I started to cry. I don't know why I laughed so hard, and for so long, but it felt so good to let go of not being afraid to follow the horse and find heaven in every step to mean flying so far away from home for the first time to teach a three day clinic in Wellington.

49

This morning, while cleaning stalls, I thought about when I lived in Thailand, and how on some mornings, if I could wake up and get out to the sludge pit of mucky water on Cheangwattana Street 31 where my flat was,

I would be able to see how being alive meant to be filled with light when the lotus flower that lived there would make the journey from the green clenched fist of a flower bud protecting itself from painful experiences

to the white open-handed-flower-blossom-like questions of someone on the path to understanding that if you don't let go, you won't grow.

50

This morning, while cleaning stalls, I thought about this horse who was afraid of falling. He was so protective of himself that when I asked him to move off of my leg, he tightened his body. So, I started singing *You Are My Sunshine*.

Someone told me that when I started singing, a little fantailed bird, that in the Māori culture symbolizes someone is about to die or an ancestor is near, flew into the arena.

When I gave the horse back to his person, she said that the song I'd just sung her horse was the song that she'd sung to her mom while she was dying.

51

This morning, while cleaning stalls, I thought about the dinner I had with Dr. Heuschmann after a panel we were on together in 2019 where he told me, among other things, to get the hardest horses I can find while I can, so they can teach me how to be of better service to the world.

I took his advice. But, sometimes I get discouraged because now I can go to a clinic and help a stranger's horse to do something in an hour that I've been working on with one of my own for over a year and still haven't achieved because of lives they'd been saved from before they came into my life.

I shared this with my horse's veterinarian when he came to give my herd their Spring shots. He said, "You're able to help other people's horses so effectively because your horses keep you so humble."

52

This morning, while cleaning stalls, I thought about acceptance as the creation out of what's left:

It's a mystery to me, but there always seems to be so many tears cried at so many of my clinics.

I'm not sure what that means.

But, this life I'm living is one of the most beautiful lives I've lived in a long time. I'm grateful of that.

53

This morning, while cleaning stalls, I thought about what it is that I believe about myself that keeps causing me to have these thoughts while I'm cleaning stalls.

And this is it, I think: I'm thankful to have a place that's safe for me to tune the rest of the world out so that I can go into my head and see some of what my mind sees in the space between the canyon walls of belief and opinion where the low-laying river of reality slithers through the world like a footpath to understanding that nothing can live inside of an energy field that won't support it.

For me, my barn is the golden city in the heart of the lotus, whose roots are my feet in the poop, and the piss, and the shavings, and whose stem is my spine rainbow-bridging my energy flanked awareness from the night to the day, and whose fragrant blossom is the opening petals of my brain bathing in the rays of early morning light.

54

This morning, while cleaning stalls, I thought about last night when I looked up at the sky and saw a horse in the stars. The horse had the wings of an angel.

There was a human being standing next to the horse. The human being had the hands of an angel.

55

This morning, while cleaning stalls, I thought about look-ing into the glazed over, unblinking eye of my neighbors old horse, Jo-jo, who died on Sunday.

Last night, before bed, I imagined Jo-jo as a few days old foal running full speed around his dam in a green field at the beginning of learning how to be in a flesh-and-blood body,

and was reminded of how we're all super magical when we're newly arrived, and our feet first touch the earth, and how the work is to stay that way as we keep walking.

56

This morning, while cleaning stalls, I thought about how horses have taught me that being a teacher means being a way along the way without getting in the way of a student's understanding of horses as the journey of trusting life enough to allow limitations to fulfill them instead of disappoint them as the key to seeing that learning is always alive for the ones who aren't in a hurry to get results in the shortest amount of time.

57

This morning, while cleaning stalls, I imagined myself as a beautiful set of seven Russian Matryoshka dolls. The fourth one, sometimes, doesn't open.

She is the one with the box in her mind that she inherited from her great-great-great grandfather on her mother's side. It's blue and has a lock and key.

It works the same as a casket. Whenever she needs to hide something that she's seen or felt, she puts it in this box in her mind, and she locks it, and those thoughts don't come anymore.

She's shy and she's afraid of everything. She's where my love for horses comes from.

58

This morning, while cleaning stalls, I thought about B., and how he's one of my most hard won and heartfelt Hallelujahs.

I woke up in the middle of the night last night while sleeping next to him with my head on his pillow, and apologized for crowding him out of his side of the bed. I said, I guess I just wanted to be close.

I moved back over to my pillow and held his hand, instead. He said, It feels like we're walking in the park. And like a dream waking up I said, I'll see you on the other side. Then closed my eyes and went back to sleep.

I thought about there being no creation without separation, and beautiful Joy Oladikun and Chris Stapleton sound singing Sweet Symphony together. Every time I listen to that song it's always one of the most beautiful moments ever.

59

This morning, while cleaning stalls, I thought about all the horses I've met who've told me that they don't want us in their lives if it means them being taken away from themselves.

I thought abut how our need for control comes from fear of losing control.

I thought about how working out of being afraid of losing control over horses is how we ask horses unsafe questions and expect horses to give us safe answers in return.

But when we unlearn how to be afraid of losing control over horses, we begin to experience how listening to horses means allowing horses to teach us how to follow their voice back to our own heart learning to see that we can only be what we are continually becoming.

60

This morning, while cleaning stalls, I thought about how following the horse and finding heaven in every step means trusting life to get me to my next step just like I trusted life to get me to the step I'm in.

I thought about how horses are teaching me to see that being is who I am, not what I do and is defined by how I spend the time I have, not the amount of time that I have to spend.

I thought about my current assignment of helping hurt horses heal from people's pasts, and how it has taught me that a broken heart is also a way to allow love to grow beyond one's physical form.

61

This morning, while cleaning stalls, I thought about death as the space between these words and letters on this page, and how each sentence is another lifetime from beginning to end.

I thought about how my mind is the sky, and how the sky is the ocean in another part of the earth.

I thought about how my soul is the ocean curling into a long arched wave and then shattering on the shore.

I thought about how my life is the high and low tide.

I thought about my body as the memory of a world where we all had to fill-in-the-blank with the personality that was created to keep us safe in the environment that we grew up in.

I thought about how the world has taught me to be addicted to my life as a legacy, and mocks me for creating an identity out of my birthright with thoughts about how my work with horses taking me to so many different places has helped me accept the English language as a beautiful gift from a barbaric past.

I thought about being as that space on the other side of letting go of time, where I'm able to see myself helping horses teach their people to trust themselves as proof of me practicing trusting myself in that moment, too.

When I don't trust myself enough, fear comes in and lets me know how far away from myself I have drifted, and fear shows me the way back to trusting myself again. Which is me learning to trust you, and me inviting you to learn to trust me, too, with the help of horses as a portal taking my energy in and recycling it back to me with the problem as time travel to how deep down the communication clot is usually rooted in an unhealed past pain.

62

This morning, while cleaning stalls, I thought about my evolution as a horseman, and how, now, I'm learning to help people find their horses by asking them to imagine a time when they felt safest in their whole life, and to conjure up that memory, and offer that feeling to the part of their horses body where the horse is tense, and then warm their horse's tight spot up until it relaxes.

In this space, the horse has been a guiding light showing me how many people don't have a point of reference for what feeling safe in their own bodies feels like.

63

This morning, while cleaning stalls, I thought about what being friends with the emotions that live around some of my hard memories looks like:

To be a human being in relationship means punishment and reward.

64

This morning, while cleaning stalls, I thought about the conversation with the Belgian guy that lives in Canada who I met at the airport in Montreal while we waited in the terminal gate to board the plane to Denver. One of the things he said that stuck with me was, "You can't choose where you're born, but you can choose where you live your life."

I thought about that time I exited onto Palmer Lake from I-25 South to go and teach one of my monthly clinics, when a Douglas County sheriff's patrol car began tailgating me.

He didn't turn his sirens on to pull me over, but was shinning his spotlight into the cab of my truck, and was so close to my back bumper that I couldn't see his grill guard in my rearview mirror.

What had happened to Philando Castile was still in the news. I began to fear for my life. I called my mom and asked her to stay on the phone so I wouldn't be alone in case anything happened to me.

The patrol car followed me for eight miles and twenty minutes until I turned right onto Highway 83 into El Paso County.

65

This morning, while cleaning stalls, I thought how I was that kid who really had a hard time growing up, and hated a lot of himself outside of his life with books and horses.

But now, those hated parts are making sense because I see that they were future parts of myself that the past part of myself didn't understand.

The past part threw those future parts away because the future parts wanted to be seen. But, the past parts weren't ready to see those future parts. Now, I'm in recovery from myself

I go to places to do my best to try and help horses and their people, only to find that those places are where the thrown away future pieces had landed. When I leave to go a place to teach, I don't come back the same person.

That piece of the question is no longer a question because

the answer has been found and added into the me that I am becoming. The brokenness is where the past that threw the shattered pieces of my future selves away is safe.

The brokenness is where the past that threw the shattered pieces of my future selves away refuses to have the courage to see that nothing is coincidence.

My work with horses has taught me how to heal my own soul-hurt places.

My work with horses has taught me how to take the power back from the part of my story that parasitic emotional pain from the past used to hold me hostage.

My work with horses has taught me that I get stuck in emotions that I fight feeling.

66

This morning, while cleaning stalls, I thought about every time I see you you're getting freer and freer.

And it's gonna be crazy because once you reach that final step, it's gonna be you setting another free by choosing not to use whatever power you have against a horse that feels like it has to protect itself from you.

You give that horse back its power, it becomes as soft as a clean cotton ball.

I thought about how the reason we make enemies is because we need them. Freedom is going to be you deciding that you don't need enemies anymore.

I thought about freedom meaning you allowing yourself to be enough. That's the only thing I've really learned how to give myself permission to be.

I thought about freedom meaning how thankful I am to have the opportunity to be very busy, but how I have to pace myself so that I can last long in my work.

I want this work to be a career, and it can only be that if I honor myself and what I need to stay healthy.

I thought about how, if I get blinded by the dollar signs in my eyeballs, and start chasing money, then I'll start making careless mistakes and horses won't trust me anymore.

67

This morning, while cleaning stalls, I thought about how, if the horse can relax, the horse will be okay. That's how I've learned to use time to rebuild broken horse hearts and broken horse bodies:

I have to not be in the horse's way to be a part of the horse's rhythm so that the work can flow like a journey back in time to the moment that the thing that haunts the horse happened. That's how the horse answers my questions, most of the time. Sometimes the horse says No.

The horse has taught me that energy follows insight like a shadow, and that my questions are clear and easier to answer when I'm not afraid to be seen. I'm not being honest with myself if I'm lying to the horse. The horse sees me as I am.

68

This morning, while cleaning stalls, I thought about how, last night, before she went to bed, my mom sent a random text message to my brother, my sister and me, part of which said, "I love you all. Nobody is perfect. I give my best. It usually works pretty well. There's always something that could be tweaked. We keep walking, figuring so many things out along the way."

69

This morning, while cleaning stalls, I thought about how I love the person that I am when I am with my horses, which is why I love my horses so much.

My horses teach me how to trust what I know.

So far, helping horses with their people as full time work has been a meditation on what I'm good at, that I can grow into me being better at by this time next year, by allowing my luck to be the effort I put into becoming who I want to be.

Now, sharing the simple lessons that my horses have shared with me has allowed me to see time as an exceeded expectation of what dreams coming true feels like, and how lonely an experience living a fulfilled life can sometimes be.

70

This evening I was walking into the barn and told my mom and J., the lady who helps keep our horses up, that I walked into my Boulder clinic this morning and the first thing I told everyone was,

"It feels like my whole world is on fire, but I'm not gonna be burned up because I've found my wings, like those Flying Africans in that old anthropology book *Drums and Shadows*.

71

This morning, while cleaning stalls, I thought about how some people only ever do what's already been done by forgetting that what they only ever do had once never ever been done before someone gained insight, changed their habits, and mastered a skill that they were then able to teach others.

I thought about how change isn't always growth.

I thought about the universe as a spiraling big band whose members play their lives in sections like beautifully tuned instruments giving birth to light:

Sometimes, I listen to the sped up NASA recordings of black holes singing deep in outer space like an echo, or the deep sea songs of blue whales serenading each other while I work with my horses in their arena.

I thought about how, now, science is confirming that the only thing to be discovered is what is already there, and how we can experience what is already there when we allow ourselves to be aware of life transcending our modern world like a prophesy.

I thought about how meditation has gotten me to the place where my mind is able to observe thought without thinking like rhythm can live without nature, and seeing that nature cannot live without rhythm.

Now, the work with my horses only happening when my horses accept the work looks like letting truth and fairness lead the way by kissing being afraid of time goodbye.

I thought about how my practice of being with horses has taught me that hurt hearts heal when hands stop doing what's not helpful.

I thought about how growth is change.

72

This morning, while cleaning stalls, I thought about training techniques that, little by little, peel horses away from themselves like a person being overtaken by Alzheimer's.

The little horse-like mind wrestling the big memory loss disease-like training technique until, eventually, the person can hardly talk and is slobbering at the table with their head

slumped over like a horse held in behind the vertical, submitting to the pain of being pulled apart after realizing they don't have any other choice.

73

This morning, while cleaning stalls, I thought about the eighty year old woman (who's been riding horses for seventy years) who came up to me with her twenty year old mare Mistletoe after their lesson in one of my monthly Boulder clinics and said:

I'm grateful you decided to be born when you decided to be born. If you would have waited any longer, I might have missed my chance to learn from you.

Not knowing what else to say, I told her: "We are all each other's gifts of grace."

74

This morning, while cleaning stalls, I thought about how the more I allow horses to exist outside of the time in my work with them, the more relaxed they stay in their work with me.

Horses don't know what time means. Horses aren't in time, but rather in that space between thoughts like a shadow between statues, where the present moment lives as the possibility of what's possible.

I thought about how there's so much that happens unnecessarily to horses just because people get bored with having enough.

I thought about how good work isn't possible if there's no one there to do it at a pace they feel safe inside of, and how each step is everything until the next step is able to be taken.

75

This morning, while cleaning stalls, I thought about how not talking to ourselves about the those parts of ourselves that we don't talk to ourselves about is the problem.

I thought about how learning to talk to ourselves about those parts of ourselves that we don't talk to ourselves about is the solution.

76

This morning, while cleaning stalls, I thought about sentience and how hard of a time so many people have with the existence of a thing without their permission.

I thought about how being with horses has taught me to re-sentientize myself by allowing myself to think and feel enough to consider my horses' thoughts and feelings about questions, and answers, and situations, and sharing space.

I thought about all of the beliefs about myself that I had to let go of to allow horses and other humans to be feeling beings in my world again.

I thought about the process of learning to trust that feeling is, and that feelings are, safe.

I thought about how it's okay to have feelings.

I thought about how once healed horses heal hurt humans, and healed humans learn to help hurt worlds, it's not fair to keep asking horses to keep healing our brokennesses over, and over again, and again, and again...

77

This morning, while cleaning stalls, I thought about watching some garter snakes hunting down crickets outside of the people-door of the barn last night, and for some reason I was reminded of how someone sent me a message that said: "You're a horse trainer who writes about training horses in quote bubbles."

I replied: That's actually how I speak... In aphorisms, like this:

When people stop using horses as an escape from life, people see that training horses is about teaching people how to change, and that the change you feel is the change that's real, and that change is the result of time and effort which is why correct practice is so important.

Or, like this:

My work has taught me that helping hurt horses get better, helps me get better, too.

These horses are the way that life is teaching me to stay as committed to the process as I am to the dream... To find the rhythm, so I don't miss the dance.

78

When I meet a new horse that asks for my help with healing their hurt, I say to them in my heart, "Hello there, you. To me, you are a flower in bloom."

In my work with them, I imagine they are a flower unfolding before my eyes, and then they start getting better.

79

This morning, while cleaning stalls,
I thought about the small silver centaur medallion
that I wear like a wizard's talisman

The mind and spirit of a human
rising out of the body of a horse
like the soul waking up from a dream of life

Life defined here
as the experience
of being half becoming whole

80

The morning, while cleaning stalls, I thought about the person who told me about how she was looking back at pictures of her riding her horse in the mountains without a care in the world, and how she thought she had to learn horsemanship techniques to not lose control over him, and how always thinking about doing x,y and z almost ruined her horse completely.

I thought about how beautiful her being accountable for doing what she did to her horse was, like the clarifying conversations after a couple has a big fight and a break up.

Why is it that we're only able to hear after the metaphorical glass lay shattered on the floor?

I thought about how when the mind is scared it creates thoughts to try and recover the parts of ourselves that we are afraid we've lost listening to what others say is best for us when it's not best for us.

I thought about how, sometimes, you don't know the value of thing until you've lost it.

81

This morning, while cleaning stalls, I thought about how ev-eryday I go to my horses looking for my particular metaphor for the interconnectedness of everything—and whose name does not matter.

And all I find is the work of seeing life opening up when I live it.

82

This morning, while cleaning stalls, I overheard me having this conversation with myself:

I want your re-memory to be so at ease that you are safe enough to be your horse's home, no matter where you are.

But first you have to be home for yourself. Do you understand?
No.

What don't you understand?
What you mean by home?

Home is where you understand who you are in your own heart, and in your own mind. It's where good things that you will hold on to forever happen.
Hmmmm.

83

This morning
while cleaning stalls
I thought about how
life is memories
and how you build good ones
like horses teaching you
the patience to teach them
how to give love
how to receive love
how love is flowing
intuitive unscripted
in the moment language
and not a play-by-play
switch to this-now-this method
full of assumptions about others
based on your own individual experiences
expecting horses to reflect
those same things back to you
instead of asking questions

84

This morning, while cleaning stalls, I thought about how horses have taught me that the language you communicate in defines who you are in a relationship, like conversational tribalism.

That said, I'm glad to have words because they make life less of a mystery. The problem usually lives in what's not said. Language comes after the hurt happens.

I thought about how the addiction to re-memories is how the body stays stuck in the minds of so many people who aren't being themselves...who are waiting for permission from me to be themselves.

But, instead of telling people how to be, like a guru, I've just decided to bring whoever wants to come along with me on my journey of becoming more of myself in the world.

85

This morning while cleaning stalls, I thought about how I was taught the horsemanship of other people, and I knew that I would never do it as well as the people I was taught to be like, and why should I attempt to do it any better? So, I began to ask the horses to lead me to the horses.

I thought about listening to me talking to myself during this dialogue:

Me- I don't want my students to trust me more than they trust themselves.

Also me- Why?

Me- When my students learn to trust themselves they learn to be themselves.

Also me- That's cool.

Me- If they trust me more than they trust themselves, they're learning to be me. We don't need a bunch more me's running around.

Me also- It's like how I don't want to be the sky, I just want
the power to throw lightening.
Me- That's a weird metaphor.
Me also- Do you trust me?
Me- Sometimes.

86

This morning, while cleaning stalls, I thought about dying and coming back as the previously unwanted horse of someone for whom horses are a best friend.

I thought about how I would really hold dear the person who showed me enough kindness to give me a home where I had as much time as I wanted to learn to trust what being loved and feeling safe long enough to stay relaxed felt like.

If, in my next life, my horses and I switch places, and I am their horse and they are my person, then I will have this gift that I've already given myself.

I try to treat people like this too. But, I must admit, almost everyone I meet confuses my heart.

87

This morning, while cleaning stalls, I thought about how she came up to me at the end of the second day of my Australia Clinic in Victoria, and said, " I remember how I asked you what the theme of your clinic tour would be when I came to see you teach in New Zealand, and you told me, 'That the world is small, but love is big.' Do you remember that?" she said. "Yes," I said. She said, "I will never forget that."

88

This morning, while cleaning stalls, I thought about how every time I look up at the clouds they show me how incredible a magician the sky is, and how the minds of mustangs are like the sky.

I thought about mustangs who've been stolen from their homelands and herds like my ancestral spirits still grieving the loss of family and friends after having been purchased off of the auction block by the highest bidder at the slave market.

I thought about how it seems to be, that for me, the key to connecting with mustangs who are having a hard time relaxing into loving human homes, is to imagine someone that I loved dearly, who was unexpectedly taken away from me, and whom I will never see again:

For me, it is one of my best friends who was twenty-two when he suicided himself sixteen years ago. After he died, I tried to put a clear question together as to why he did it. Only to realize that I would never find an answer that was the truth, because the only person who could give it to me has decided to go away forever. It's really shitty when someone else's choice breaks your heart so badly.

My mare, Mohawk, taught me this exercise, and that in each moment we choose either to see or not to see that we live out of the spaces we think we can live in, and that sometimes peace comes from forgiving someone who will never apologize, and that all of it is love, and that all love matters.

I offered Mohawk's exercise to a student whose mustang mare would run around on the lead rope in a desperate search for safety like she was being chased with a lunge whip. When the student recalled the memory of a lost loved one, the mare stopped, took a long full-body breath, faced her person, lowered her head, laid down in the deep arena sand, then got up and licked-and-chewed before following her person out of the gate like a dear and trusted friend.

89

This morning, while cleaning stalls, I thought about what I'd
like anyone who chooses to learn from me to know, and it's
this:

I want to make something very clear to you
I'm here to help you, okay
And listen to me
And I really want you to understand this
I don't have any expectation
Beyond you letting me know how I can help you
And you helping me help you if I'm able to
So if the nervousness stems from you feeling like
You have to answer questions that are too big
That is not why I'm here
Do you understand
Now what I would really like for you to do first
Is to find your breath

90

This morning, while cleaning stalls, I thought about how my life with horses has defined love as a skill that must be developed with the discipline it takes to enjoy being together.

91

This morning, while cleaning stalls, I thought about how my friend, Tamar Reno, sent me an email a while back about the Omaha word for horse. And so I sent her a message asking if I could include it in this collection of meditations. She agreed.

Here it is:

The Omaha word for horse is Shónge.

The first part of the word, Shón is an adverb, and can be translated as "still" or "continually."

The second part of the word is ge, which indicates "scattered." In Omaha, nouns are usually followed by a particle called a positional (in this case ge). The positional adds dynamic to the noun.

(Unlike English, which is a static language, many Indigenous languages are dynamic. There's motion in the language).

When I think about Shónge, I think of the horses continually calling us, the scattered, into the sacred.

92

This morning, while cleaning stalls, I thought about how the most important key to connection for me is that my horse feels as safe inside of my question as I feel safe inside of my question.

And so the real question is: Do I feel safe?

What does that mean?

It means you have to feel safe enough to not feel like you have to earn feeling safe. You don't need anyone's permission to feel safe.

What does that mean?

It means that you don't need to teach the horse to be safe if you offer the horse safety that the horse can believe in.

93

This morning, while cleaning stalls, I thought about how my work with horses cannot come from a memory of having my power taken away from me.

Then, I'm not addressing the horse's problem as a problem to be fixed and it ceases being a problem, because there's nothing left in me for the horse to balance the problem on.

Connection is acceptance, I think, and acceptance is the creation out of what's left.

94

This morning, while cleaning stalls, I thought about how humans have created a world where we are almost so hopelessly divided, and that we have to live with it, but that we soon won't be able to live with much longer.

I thought about how horses offering themselves as a bridge to help us heal the worlds we used them to conquer is what's gonna save horses in our attempt to save ourselves.

I thought about my body as the earth, and this precious human birth, and how when people don't take our need to always be at war into the places where we go to find peace, then so much will change.

I thought about how I've seen people change when they feel safe enough to feel something, like my Grandman who quit a sixty year cigarette smoking habit (cold turkey) after receiving a diagnosis of terminal cancer in his lungs that quickly spread to his brain.

95

This morning, while cleaning stalls, I thought about what Yoda-pony has taught me about 1+1=1 relationships.

If you're not better than me without you, then you can keep walkin'.

It's the inhale to my exhale and the exhale to my inhale or nothin'.

96

This morning, while cleaning stalls, I thought about how I learned to ride horses across the street from the county jail in the middle of the city,

and how, when the world is not safe, horses are my safest place in the world.

I thought about how my horses stay with me the closer I stay to my heart.

I thought about how, if I'm all for giving the horse the time that it needs, then I have to be all for giving myself the time that I need, too,

so that I don't have to build a life around a space I can't show up in.

97

This morning, while cleaning stalls, I was thought about how grateful I am for everything when I heard the people door to the barn close. So, I looked out and saw my mom walking down the isle to see her cats in their room across from Mohawk's stall.

I said: *Good morning!*
She said: Good morning.
I said: *How are you?*
She said: I'm I AM.

98

This morning, while cleaning stalls, I thought about a conversation I had with another horse trainer about whether or not a horse can give a human consent, and agree to do something.

This particular trainer didn't think they could.

I told them how I think the power of the ego lay in the fear of losing control of the illusion of one's self as a real, permanent, fixed thing that really exists and will be remembered.

And how I think not feeling like a horse can choose, lay in a person feeling like there are parts of themselves that can be taken away without their permission. Because of that, they are creating a slave out of feeling like they have the power to give another sentient being permission to feel.

All of this, I think, stems from feeling like we need to earn the right to feel safe.

99

This morning, while cleaning stalls, I listened to a robin trilling from one of the trees.

When I'm away from my horses for too long I feel like a song without a singer.

My horses are a better-than-any-mirror reflection of me when I'm with them.

My life as their person is helping me see that connection means knowing I'm never alone.

100

This morning, while cleaning stalls, I thought about the correct choice being the difficult choice as a way to pinpoint fear, like when my horses aren't doing something that I want them to do.

And I ask myself, "Do I have the courage to cultivate a friendship with my horse that's as deep, in it's own way, as the friendship that my horse has cultivated with other horses?"

That takes courage to see how Nova shows up for Remi, or how Dancer shows up for Mohawk, and how Yoda-pony shows up for himself. It takes courage to understand how easy it is to see success and not know the story behind what you're seeing: the process of suffering constructively for your goals and dreams.

I thought about why they feel so safe with who they feel safe with, and what they can teach me about being such a safe space for another, because an open heart is a heart that's able to love more and that's what all of us need, and so I asked them.

Nova said: Be kind.

Mohawk said: Be steady.

Dancer and Remi both said: Be trustworthy.

Yoda-pony said: Everything that everyone else said plus, don't forfeit yourself.

101

Last night, I dreamed about a red mare. She was very sick. I told her that the only way she could heal was by learning to dream. She could not do it and died.

I woke up from the dream not knowing what the dream meant.

When you wake up, you know you were sleep.

102

This morning, while cleaning stalls, I thought about these words that Xodo woke me up from my sleep at 1 A.M. singing:

Nahshon, I want you to help me until the end of time.
I feel safe enough to relax and be myself around you.
You understand that I shut down when I don't feel safe.
I feel like I've found you much too late my life:
I've already spent most of my strength on the past.
All I can give you is the little best effort I have left,
Hoping it's enough for you to stay and help me until the end of time.

Hope: The work I do with Xodo that separates new meaning and bad memories.

103

This morning, while cleaning stalls, I thought about Toni Morrison's 1993 Noble speech and how it helped me understand that language is relationship, that safety and trust are belonging, and that belonging is connection.

Below is what the work of me learning to let horses help them heal has taught me about being in relationship so far:

I'm better when you see me.

If we only go as far into the question as we both feel safe, how far can we get together?

104

This morning, while cleaning stalls, I thought about how my energy influences how my horse feels about the space we're in together,

and how safety is the horse knowing that they're better with me when they're with me.

That's the heart of every relationship that's safe.

I thought about how safety's an easy thing to sculpt a healthy boundary out of:

I'm safer with you than I am alone: you're a good thing for me.

I'm not safer with you than I am alone: you're not a good thing for me. You're not healthy for my life.

I'm safer with you than I am alone, that's community: that's partnership. What a gift it is to be able to find that.

105

This morning, while cleaning stalls, I thought about how my horses have taught me how important it is to give myself room to grow, because anything that's real has to leave room for the possibility of growth.

I can't live like a plant potted in a pot that's too small, with roots that are all mashed up because there's no more room for them to stretch their legs, and so they're all tangled and knotted up like a wet 4C afro. But, if you put the plant in a bigger pot the roots stretch out their legs.

Growth is life.

106

This morning, while cleaning stalls, I thought about when Warwick Schiller got in touch with me for an interview, the interview that opened so much more of the world up to my work with horses.

It took me a few days to respond. I wasn't sure what I wanted to do.

When I told my mom about my dilemma, she asked if I felt like I deserved for my dreams to come true.

When I was fourteen, I told one of my riding instructors about the dream of being able to make a living helping horses be happier in the human world.

My riding instructor laughed at me and said, "Good Luck."

107

Someone asked me if in my travels I've seen any differences between horse people around the world.

I said, "People think people are different, but horses know people aren't different."

That's why I trust horses more than I trust people.

But, in my lessons, what I'm learning from people is that when I try and get them to trust themselves by asking them what I can help them with, and we work exploring out of that space,

then they're not able to give their power away, and, for one reason or another, they aren't afraid to let their horses have rest breaks from the work.

108

This morning, while cleaning stalls, I thought about how we're all going to be forgotten.

The world is a dark room.

I am a light. You are a light.

Shine.

109

This morning, while cleaning stalls, I thought about how once, at the end of one of my clinics, a guy came up to me and said, "Hey Nahshon, for the last few months my life has been in shambles, and I had planned on killing myself, down to deciding who my horses were gonna go to.

"But, I held off when I saw that you were coming to see if I could get any insight that could offer me perspective. And I did! The clouds have begun to clear, and I just wanted to come up and tell you thanks for being you."

110

This morning, while cleaning stalls, I thought about how life is so beautiful, and how life is so not fair.

I thought about how, one day during a lesson the little mustang mare, Arrow, told me that the only difference between being powerful and being strong is that being powerful happens when you believe in yourself.

111

This morning, while cleaning stalls, I thought about how once at a clinic I was sitting on this beautiful little eleven year old retired brood mare for the second time in just as many days, when she began showing me how her heart had been broken into seven pieces that she'd never feel beat again because they'd been sold and sent off to the highest bidder by the breeder as weanlings;

how her head had been secured to a post and her hind legs locked to the ground with breeding hobbles so that she could be safely covered by a stallion.

I thought about how Yoda-pony once told me how, sometime, it takes a long time to trust people again.

Then the mare asked me to get off because she didn't feel like having anyone else on her back right now—and never without her permission ever again.

So I got off, handed her back to her person, and shared what she'd just told me."

112

This morning, while cleaning stalls, I thought about flying from this-to-that country at such a high frequency between time zones as I have been lately, has begun to make it feel like the earth is its own parallel multiverse;

where, no matter where I go, I see that horses are always horses; and that people are always wishing and working and paying for the same, more beautiful, life with their horses in so many different ways:

In the morning, sparrows.
In the evening, crows.

113

This morning, while cleaning stalls, I stopped cleaning for a bit and and just gave Yoda-pony a big hug around his little fuzzy, grey Yoda-pony neck.

Before I continued on to Mohawk's stall, I asked Yoda-pony to tell me something beautiful.

Yoda-pony said, "No less fear, just more fearless."

114

This morning, while cleaning stalls, I thought about how healthy horse herds are full of boundaries, and honest questions, and honest answers balancing truth like the real thing;

and how much more magically enchanting horses really are when they aren't romanticized like a fairy queen of the forest.

I thought about consciousness as a human idea that sometimes feels like a bad joke nature is telling about my mind.

I thought about how horses have taught me that seeing reality means seeing when things change, or don't change.

115

This morning, while cleaning stalls, I thought about how if I want you to trust me as a teacher, more that I want you, as a student, to trust yourself, then I'm trying to turn you into me,

which is misguided and abusive, and is pretty indicative of a lack of self-worth on my part, as a teacher, with an over inflated ego.

I thought about how the purpose of the ego is to be afraid of being forgotten.

I thought about how my dreams are still bigger than my fears, and how my dreams coming true should not be a nightmare for you.

I thought about how the more of me I am as your teacher, the more permission I give you, as my student, to be yourself too.

The more of yourself you are, the more of yourself you learn to be. The more of yourself you learn to be, the more of yourself you are.

I thought about how being with horses has taught me that I always am, and that I always was, and that I always will be a horseman: neither just a horse, or only a man.

116

This morning, while cleaning stalls, I thought about the answer I gave to the person at one of my clinics who asked me where I was actually from, as if she was expecting me to tell them something other than what I told them, which was this:

I'm not going to answer that question anymore, because the answer doesn't really matter.

I've found more-and-more that, sometimes, people ask me questions to see why I can do what I can do as a reason for why they can't.

I trust myself… I trust myself…and every lesson in this whole clinic has been about what happens when we trust ourselves…

The changes that happen when we feel what we feel and we know that it's real enough not to doubt.

I refuse to be made into an exotic thing by not making myself into what others want me to be, and I'm inviting people to do the same for themselves:

To be wholly who they are in the world by ceasing to be who they're not. And we see how their horses have changed for the better, in their bodies and their minds, when that happens.

Horses are my light; they are my connection to you and they are my connection to heaven, and they are proof to me that those two things are one in the same.

Otherwise, it feels like I walk though the world like some freak show that people look at because I'm a shiny thing, and since all I see is myself in you, I don't know how to see you as not possible for yourself, too. It's my blessing and my curse.

117

This morning, while cleaning stalls, I thought about how each life is a world.

I thought about a former client who was so addicted to drama that when their horse was calm, they'd create a storm and make their horse crazy, again, because they needed something to do.

Towards the end, every time I walked into the arena for my lesson with them and their horse, it felt like I was carrying a coffin on my back.

I thought about how that person didn't allow me to know how to else to help them be better for their horse. And so, since I'm a simple horseman and not a psychologist, I had to let them and their horse go.

118

This morning while cleaning stalls, I thought about the horses I've chosen who I'd chosen to buy who didn't choose me back.

The common theme amongst them all is I bought them for show and not for connection, and showing was not my goal.

I didn't realize it then, but their rejection of me took my power away. To get my power back, I studied training methods that I thought would make them interested in me. That never happened.

So I found the people that my horses wanted to be with, and allowed their lives together to be possible.

When I met the horses I have now, they all told me, each in their own way, that I was their person and that they wanted to be my horses, and that we were meant to be together.

I told them each, "Ok. Show me the way to make it happen, and I will."

119

This morning, while cleaning stalls, I thought about how my sister was out yesterday, and saw me and Nova chillin' in the field, came up, and just started taking pictures.

I closed my eyes and smiled, secretly hoping the whole impromptu photo shoot to be over soon. It was.

When she sent me the photos last night, I saw the one that summed up my life so beautifully, in that it shows me dressed in a dusty pair of blue jeans, and my pink, long sleeved t-shirt that has Good Trouble written on the front of it.

I have a durag on my head to protect my hair from getting damaged by the dust and by the sun.

Nova is standing behind me, grazing. I'm sitting cross legged inside of his shadow, my most safest safe space in the whole world.

My sister called me this evening, while I was tying hay bags. Before she hung up, I told her thanks for capturing such a beautiful moment.

120

This morning, while cleaning stalls, I thought about how instead of examining my heart while sitting on a yoga mat with closed eyes, I shovel shit and shavings into a muck bucket.

This form of meditation has become the salve healing the disease of my addiction to the story.

I'm finding that the disease of being addicted to the story empowers the problem. Empowered problems are hard to solve.

I thought about how the disease of being addicted to the story never misses an opportunity to miss an opportunity to do better and be better

like an uncontrollable downwards spiral into inter-generational wars of emotional tribalism helping me see what I do and don't want be in the land of the living, and how that journey is transitioning me out of personhood and into a human being bringing what they are into alignment with who they are like a ladyboy.

I thought about how being alive makes me feel so beautifully human.

I thought about how the more human I feel, the more of a horseman I become, and how being a horseman, to me, means allowing a horse to be so special that I see myself in the horse, and that I love the horse so deeply because the horse is me learning how to love myself in relationship with people responding to others in time.

I thought about how time is the fear of running out of time as a definition for perfection.

I thought about how horses have introduced me to so many people who are frozen cold in life by perfection.

I thought about perfection as a horse being shut down by a person who has been shut down.

I thought about how perfection is rigor mortis like a eulogy at a funeral, which is always for other people.

I thought about how other people have taught me how to suffer by me trusting other people more than I trust myself.

I thought about love.   I thought about love.   I thought about love.

And I thought about pizza.

121

This morning, while cleaning stalls, I thought how much I love my Yoda-pony. So, I put my muck fork down and went to check in with him in his paddock:

Me: How are you?
Yoda-pony: Do you have time to listen to my answer.

Me: Of course.
Yoda-Pony: I've been here before, but I've not been here today. So, good morning, and welcome to the story of my life.

Look! The sun.

122

This morning, while cleaning stalls, I thought about how at her first lesson she said she'd seen her teacher, who had died some years ago, in me. Her former teacher had died from riding a client's horse who'd flipped over backwards on him. She'd studied with him for many years.

She said that my work gave her hope for horses and their people, and she thanked me for coming. I told her thank you and said, "You're welcome."

On her second day's lesson, there was a ghost who'd walked into the arena with her.

When I told her that I could feel the ghost in my heart, her neck stiffened, and her left shoulder sunk down two inches lower than her right shoulder.

For some reason, when she walked into the arena with her horse she'd just let her horse loose, and her horse would only let her rub its rump.

As time passed, and the lesson unfolded, I told her that I kept feeling like the block between her and her horse had to do with the heaviness she was holding in her heart.

A few moments after I said that, the ghost had taken my heart in its hand and clinched it tightly with a quick squeeze, like a stress ball during a panic attack.

The muscles under my left scapula jerked closed in contraction so quickly, and with such force, that my left side collapsed. I was nearly dropped to my knees. I thought I was having a heart attack. Up to this point, she'd tried not to look at me.

So, I got the horse's halter, put it on the horse and asked her what her horse was protecting her from.

She broke down in tears and said, "It was my horse (not this one) who flipped over and killed my teacher."

123

This morning, while cleaning stalls, I thought about how I saw a yellow shooting star galloping across the sky like an iron flash

last night on my way down to the barn where my horses munched on their hay as if they were receiving all of the love and happiness from the whole world.

Before I became their person, all of my horses suffered badly. Now, they're each a rainbow bodied poem that I'm learning to word wisely.

Here's a Yoda-pony poem:
Human behavior is a whip.

Here's a Remi poem:
Your gut shares information with you that your brain won't pass through. Trust your gut, always.

Here's a Dancer poem:
Just be you. Don't be afraid to embody the magic that you know.

Here's a Mohawk poem:
The love someone has for you is the love someone has for you.

Here's a Nova poem:
You make yourself real by telling the truth.
Tell the truth, and take good care of yourself.

124

This morning while cleaning stalls
Yoda-pony told me

Horse training methods
Are horses

Laughing at humans
For not seeing more

Where do you start
You start with surrender

125

This morning, while cleaning stalls, I watched as Yoda-pony stood in his paddock eating breakfast from his hay bale bag with closed eyes. After some time, Yoda-pony's magpie friend flew in, landed, and began pecking manure from beneath Yoda-pony's left front heel bulb, and I thought to myself "This is how relationship works.":

trust how it makes you feel
if it feels like home
make it home
if you can

126

This morning, while cleaning stalls, I thought about horses as a scapegoat for the human addiction to not feeling unprocessed past pain

in hopes of disappearing long deflected fears of having to be an accountable inner-adult beautifully re-landscaping their brain

with an inner-child who's receiving unconditional love from healthy role models

living out the management of their own imperfections in a life-sustaining way.

127

This morning, while cleaning stall, I thought about how embodying not needing to protect myself from horses is what it feels like for me to have an open heart. Having an open heart is how I've learned to invite horses into a partnership with me that's safe enough to relax inside of:

Once, Vern, a Morgan I work with, explained to me that he likes our lessons because I do things with him, not to him.

I thought about what Vern told me when, the other day, a friend asked what partnership means to me: I said, "When I can give you my beating heart, with the key that unlocks all the buttons to break it, and you don't."

128

This morning, while cleaning stalls, I thought about James Baldwin, hyphenated-Americans, and Chis Stapleton reverently lullabying the National Anthem at Super Bowl Fifty-seven.

I thought about trying to help in the way people are asking me to help, and the parts of my practice that I would feel safe enough to mass produce in video form and sell without the fear of a horse being hurt by the purchase.

I shared that concern with one of my students who reminded me of how I once told her: "The problems you're having with your horse are you running from you."

She said, "That's where I was stuck, until you helped me get myself unstuck. You could teach other teachers how to teach that, Nahshon."

I thought about how I believe in horses and humans more than I do in new techniques and old traditions of horsemanship. I thanked her for her belief in me, too.

I thanked her, also, for listening to me realize that I'm using my fear of saying something to another person that would cause a horse to be harmed for not being able to fit inside of one of my sentences as a mask to hide from my struggle of internalizing my, mostly successfully sharing, of a good thing in my clinics to help horses with their people.

She said, "Making some of your ideas more easily available to more people in this way is the next step across the bridge from you being who you are doing what you love, to you blossoming into who you are becoming by allowing what you love to love you back.

129

This morning, while cleaning stalls, I thought about the one day Yoda-pony was set to go back to where he came from when he told me he didn't want to leave.

The following evening, I called the person who left him for me to work with and told them that Yoda-pony told me he wanted to stay.

When I shared with them that I'd told Yoda-pony he'd have to figure a way to make what he wanted to happen work, they told me that morning, they'd woken up from a dream in which them and Yoda-pony were facing each other in a bubble, when a little light blue dot made its way though the middle of the bubble and split them and Yoda-pony apart.

I thought about how, a year prior to his arrival, I received a call from them. We'd never met, or talked before; but still, they wanted to know whether or not I thought Yoda-pony should be should be put to death due to his deep distrust of people, and his then person, not honestly knowing what else to do to help him, or at least not hurt him anymore.

Yoda-pony began to trust me when he felt that I saw how hard it was for him to trust me, and decided that his life was with me and my life was with him. So, here we are.

130

This morning, while cleaning stalls, I thought about a lady that took a lesson with me the other day. I complimented her for a job well done. She crassly responded with self-depreciation.

I asked why she kept throwing herself face first into the sand every time I gave her a compliment.

Instead of answering the question, she began hyperventilating and said she was having an anxiety attack.

I told her I have anxiety attacks, too, when I find myself in healthy situations that I'm not sure how to grow into.

I told her how I'm seeing that when confronted about self-deprecation, she goes into an anxiety attack and uses both as an excuse for why she can't reach her riding goals.

I asked her to decide how helpful her excuses were for our lesson.

And just like that, the hyperventilating stopped, her face cleared up, the tears and snot stopped flowing, as if the "Off" switch had been flicked.

A miracle!

I asked her, "What do you want to do?

She said, "To trot."

I said, "Go trot, but let your mare's reins out a little so that she can come over her back."

She did it brilliantly.

131

This morning, while cleaning stalls, I thought about freezing and falling off my horse because I began thinking about how hurt I could get if I fall, and how dangerous riding horses has become.

Now, I'm afraid to get back on my horse. But, I love riding so much. It's so frustrating. I love riding so much, but I'm scared to try it, again.

It used to be that my mind loved when my heart shared her dreams, and my heart loved it when my mind shard his thoughts.

Now, my mind and my heart speak different languages and don't understand each other anymore, like two friends who've grown apart.

132

This morning, while cleaning stalls, I thought about how there is always a beautiful flower garden of faces and hearts in the places I go to teach.

It often makes me think about how universal the reach of horses is for people who swear how different they are from each other, but aren't.

There's this common hoofed-thread running through the seams of all of our lives that's stitching us together in love for horses.

It's my prayer that people's love for horses, turns into people's love for themselves, and each other.

133

This morning, while cleaning stalls, I thought about how the work with my horses is teaching me to see emotion as the nakedness beneath all of the layers I wear like clothes,

and to see feel as all of those layers having been taken off and looking in the mirror at the nakedness staring back at me with much more kindness, and compassion, and mercy.

Emotion happens when I'm hiding.
Feel happens when I'm not hiding.

I think that the next step being found by trusting life is what it means to live.

I think that the ground being found by trusting the fall is what it means to heal.

When life breaks my ego or love breaks my heart, I suffer, I learn, and I grow into more of myself by turning pain into light.

134

This morning, while cleaning stalls, I thought about the work of learning to see how beautiful human beings are beneath all of the baggage as a butterfly eating a way out of its cocoon before loping around the air with pretty patterned wings like forgiveness letting go.

135

This morning, while cleaning stalls, I thought about how learning to keep the pigeons out of the horse's barn by trying to see the barn from the pigeon's point of view is really helping me understand how the answer to the problem is found in the problem.

136

This morning, while cleaning stalls,
I thought about the small silver centaur medallion
that I wear like a wizard's talisman

The mind and spirit of a human
rising out of the body of a horse
like the soul waking up from a dream of life

Life defined here
as the experience
of being half becoming whole

137

This morning, while cleaning stalls, I listened to Fannie Lou Hamer sing *All The Pretty Little Horses* over and over again while I thought about how, last night, my sleep was a black sky being flown around in by equid-angels.

Light in darkness.

138

This morning, while cleaning stalls, I listened to Lee Williams & the Spiritual QCs sing *Wave My Hands* on repeat for two hours as I meditated on how freedom means forgiving life's hurts like Christ on the Cross embodying beautifully the Buddha's teaching on non-attachment.

Non-attachment defined, for me, as the practice of letting life, and its happenings, come and go without judgement or force, or being afraid, like meditation. Meditation is the posture of peace.

I thought about how the end of suffering means knowing how to suffer, with a deep love, and passion, and care for life by engaging deeply with, and trusting, life. Like the poem *The Journey* by Mary Oliver.

Then, life becomes trustworthy to be what life is, which is changing...always changing...That life, when lived, is change. Life is change. Change is changeless. For me, this is salvation.

139

This morning, while cleaning stalls, I listened to Fanny Lou Hammer sing All The Pretty Little Horses over and over again, while I thought about equestrianism as my energetic awareness in partnership with the horse's movement.

To me, being relaxed while riding means forgetting about form, and just following the horse!

140

This morning, while cleaning stalls, I thought about a sad horse who'd come into the arena with his very sad young person. During the course of their introduction, the horse's person had shared how the horse was only eleven years old and was getting injections in nine of his joints, and how the veterinarians couldn't really figure out the origin of all of the little gelding's lamenesses.

The horse's person went on to share how the horse had a tendency to be super-duper tight on his right side. So, I asked if could sit on him to try and see if could figure out what was going on.

After I'd gotten in the saddle, I felt in my lower back that his lower back was so super-duper tight on the right side, that the right saddle of his saddle was super-duper lifted up, and the left side of his saddle was really dropped low.

As I'm riding this beautiful little gelding around with heated up healing energy in my lower back to relax and even out his back, I'm listening with my body to what his body is telling me. I pick up that the energy of the person who gave his body those bad memories belonged to a mean-hearted man who hurts horses for no reason like a demon disrespecting life.

I shared this information with the horse's person after she got back on her beautiful little gelding, then asked if she knew the man that I was talking about in regards to the memory that her horse's body was holding like heartbreak as a safe space. She said that she did.

When the horse's person began talking about this trainer, she began to weep, and the right side of the horse's body reverted to contraction, just like at the beginning of the lesson. Then I asked the horse's person to stop with the story, and to just ride her beautiful little gelding, and the right side of the horse's body softened back into symmetry again.

One of the chief concerns that the beautiful little gelding's person told me she had about her horse, was that his hocks would always touch. But, though out the course of prompting the horse's person to intentionally change the story that she rode her horse with, and by teaching her how to move energy through her body, by the end of the lesson we'd heated and loosened the beautiful little gelding's psoas muscles up. So much so, that when halted, he was square, and his hocks where hips-width apart.

I thought about how being with horses helps me remember that everything in everything. But how really scary things still happen sometimes, and I forget to see the oneness of it all, and become very small like love passing as anger to try and save itself from being disappeared by life. I'm still unlearning how to be afraid.

141

This morning, while cleaning stalls, I thought about how it, sometimes, feels like there's a kill pen full of horses hoping for help in my mind.

Their pain is the past catching up with the future, and coming harder than thought possible, like a mother whose child you've hurt.

142

This morning, while cleaning stalls, I thought about self-growth meaning the worst that I am being better than the worst than I was when Yoda-pony walked out into the barn aisle, and to the closed arena door before he stopped, and looked back at me like, "I'm ready to work, now."

143

This morning, while cleaning stalls, I thought about the life I'm building out of my work until I rested my muck fork against the wall, got down on my knees, and conferred this blessing upon myself:

May your hands follow your heart as your soul follows the horse into the depths of understanding relationship as people being aware of themselves in the lives of others so that no one is left alone.

May your hands follow your heart as your soul follows the horse into the depths of understanding success as a constant struggle to keep your essence and your actions in alignment with love.

May your hands follow your heart as your soul follows the horse into the depths of understanding that impossibility is usually the projection of the worst on a situation.

You will continue to see with fresh eyes for as long as you listen. Listening is possibility. Possibility is the validation of life. Life is learning.

May your hands follow your heart as your soul follows the horse into the depths of understanding that playing it safe doesn't mean being comfortable. But rather, getting what can get done, done. That's how you grow. Don't be afraid to grow... Don't be afraid to make mistakes... Keep growing...

144

This morning, while cleaning stalls, I thought about two beautiful things my little herd of equid-angels has taught me, so far. Here they are:

1) Troubles don't last always. But, sometimes, trauma does stay a while.

2) Healing is the practice of allowing love to be bigger than bad memories.

145

This morning, while cleaning stalls, I thought about how my horses are the beat to my heart.

146

This morning, while cleaning stalls, I thought about how my art as a horseman can only be sculpted out of aids that the horse will accept.

147

This morning, while cleaning stalls, I thought about how when I begin cleaning stalls, I am a slave to my mind. When I finish cleaning stalls, both me and my mind are free. The ritual act of cleaning stalls is like a devotee caring for the alter of a deity for me. The daily practice of cleaning stalls Is meditation for my mind.

It's usually while cleaning stalls that my mind does its best thinking. In the daily training of my horses, I use stalls as a lesson in aloneness not being forever: In the morning, they're let out of their stalls, they spend all day, every day, together. Then, in the evening, it's, once again, back to their stalls. This predictability is good for my horses thinking:

I don't want my horses to be afraid of stalls or anything else that could help them in their life. I once watched a gelding who was afraid of stalls die of colic during an emergency wildfire evacuation. His person said he'd never been trained to stalls. And since belief is, indeed, an education I use their arena, their trailer, and their stalls to do the best I can to prepare my horse for their life.

148

This morning, while cleaning stalls, I remembered beginning to feel warm tingling around the pins that the doctor put in my hand to piece the broken bone in my thumb back together again, before I was awakened from sleep this morning, at seven-o-clock, by a flock of frantic squawking in the backyard. So I got out of bed, looked out of the window, and saw a Northern Goshawk in the low cut weeds, behind the deck, using its talons to squeeze the life out of a little red breasted American robin whose choir of feathered friends seemed to be trying to sing it free from being breakfast.

My herd had their farrier appointment that day, which wound up turning into a meditation for me on how what you love loves you back: When it was each of my equid's turn to get their toes trimmed, they all just dropped their head down into their halter like a holstered gun. All I had to do was slide the crown piece behind their ears and latch the jaw-strap before walking them to the barn aisle, where they each stood with the patience, and clarity, of a saint's gaze while they received their pedicures.

I had to have a plastic bag, up to my wrist, over the hand of my slinged arm so that the ace bandage wrap and surgical dressing wouldn't get dirty. I've never spent time teaching my horses how not to be afraid of plastic bags, or taught them how to halter themselves. But they knew that I was hurt and they chose to do what they could to help me while I'm broken and bruised, just like I did for them when our roles were reversed.

149

This morning, while cleaning stalls, I thought about how my work has convinced me that my horses are not horses, but angels sent from the most beautiful corner of heaven,

and how the most important lesson my work with my herd has taught me so far has been this:

The more simple and unselfish my motivation for working with my horses is, the deeper my connection to my horses is.

150

This morning, while cleaning stalls, I thought about the lady in New York who asked if I had any insight into a possible way to help her unridden mare properly engage her thoracic sling.

After I told her that a lowered sweet iron snaffle could likely do it, she said she didn't use bits because they reminded her of the Scold's bridle-like iron bit used to keep slaves from speaking as punishment by their owners way, way, way back when.

I'd never heard that reason given for working a horse bitless before.

"I don't know what else I can say," I told her, before I thanked her for her question, then turned around and walked away thinking about how empathy sometimes triggers ancestral re-memories of moments when being alive hurt so badly that not even so much spent time could heal it.

That evening, in my hotel room, I sat journaling about a lesson I had a week before with someone who studies my work with me. After he'd gotten in the saddle, before the lesson began, he said this, and I'm paraphrasing:

"I'm starting to understand that the purpose of this part of my life is me learning to be the best lover of myself that I can be. Our horses and our dogs are bringing the people into our lives that are helping me do that."

I shared how my mom once told me that, "People are people. People will break your heart. As long as you know that, you'll be okay."

I told them how I think human beings help people's hearts heal, like angels, and how I think we're all both human beings and people in equal measure. We help and we hurt. One is the beat of the other's heart.

"I think that's a beautiful, whole definition for relationship," I concluded.

151

This morning, while cleaning stalls, I thought about how I should include this meditation that I wrote last Sunday evening after my clinic:

This afternoon at lunch, I told the old man how it feels like the horse's body is my Bible, the horse's movement is my scripture, and how my work with horses is my prayer.

This evening, after the clinic had ended, I told the old man how I really don't know what I would do without horses in my life.

The old man said, "Keep staying worthy of them, and they'll keep showing up."